AF225744

Accounting for Cryptocurrency

Steven M. Bragg

ISBN 978-1-64221-221-1

For more information about AccountingTools® products, visit our Web site at www.accountingtools.com.

Table of Contents

About the Author

Steven Bragg, CPA, has been the chief financial officer or controller of four companies, as well as a consulting manager at Ernst & Young. He received a master's degree in finance from Bentley College, an MBA from Babson College, and a Bachelor's degree in Economics from the University of Maine. He has been a two-time president of the Colorado Mountain Club, and is an avid alpine skier, mountain biker, and certified master diver. Mr. Bragg resides in Centennial, Colorado. He has written more than 300 books and courses, including *New Controller Guidebook*, *GAAP Guidebook*, and *Payroll Management*.

Steven maintains the accountingtools.com web site, which contains continuing professional education courses, the Accounting Best Practices podcast, and thousands of articles on accounting subjects.

Buy Additional AccountingTools Courses

AccountingTools offers more than 1,500 hours of CPE courses, with concentrations in accounting, auditing, finance, taxation, and ethics. Related courses that you might like include:

- Accounting for Investments
- Foreign Currency Accounting
- Payables Management

Go to accountingtools.com/cpe to view these additional courses.

Accounting for Cryptocurrency

Introduction

There is a great deal of worldwide interest in acquiring or mining cryptocurrencies, but there is little information available about how to account for them. In this manual, we cover the basics of cryptocurrency, and then address the fundamental accounting associated with it.

Cryptocurrency Basics

In this section, we cover the basics of cryptocurrency, including its nature, the blockchain, the cryptocurrency wallet, cryptocurrency exchanges, and several related issues.

The Nature of Cryptocurrency

Cryptocurrency is any form of currency that exists digitally and uses cryptography to secure transactions. Cryptocurrencies use a decentralized system to record transactions and issue new units; there is no central issuing or regulating authority. A digital currency is one that only exists in a digital format, so it has no tangible representation – such as bills or coins.

What is Cryptography?

So, why is digital currency called *crypto*currency? Does it have anything to do with cryptography? *Cryptography* is a method of protecting information and communications through the use of codes, so that only those for whom the information is intended can read and process it. It is derived from mathematical concepts and a set of rule-based calculations to transform information in ways that are hard to decipher.

Despite the name, a blockchain does not have to be encrypted through the use of cryptography. This information is both available to the public and auditable. However, encryption can be used to obscure the data stored within a blockchain.

The main reason for the use of crypto within the cryptocurrency term is that encryption is used to sign messages sent to the blockchain. The information within these messages needs to be kept private, since they initiate transactions and updates to the blockchain ledger.

The Blockchain

A *blockchain* is a distributed database that is shared among the nodes[1] of a computer network. Each of these nodes contains a copy of the database, and they stay in sync

---

[1] A *node* is a computer that receives and validates transactions and blocks. The nodes in a network ensure that it operates properly. A node can involve nothing more than a desktop computer, or it can be a more specialized hardware device.

by routinely communicating with each other. If the network finds that invalid transactions are being sent from a particular node, it can throw away these transactions and block the node from which they were sent. Therefore, it is essentially impossible for anyone to corrupt the underlying data.

A blockchain collects information into groups, known as blocks. The storage capacity in a block is capped, so once a block is filled, it is closed and linked to the previously-filled block, resulting in a chain of data (hence the name). Data received subsequent to this block are compiled into a new block that will also be added to the blockchain once it has been filled. A key element of a blockchain is that it guarantees the fidelity of the stored data, resulting in a high level of trust without the need for a trusted third party to operate it.

Blockchains can be used for any type of data storage at all, but are primarily known for their role in the operation of cryptocurrency systems, so that transaction records are stored in a secure and decentralized manner. This means that a blockchain might store data about who received cryptocurrency, how much they now have, and how much they have transferred to others. Therefore, from an accounting perspective, it can be considered a ledger of transactions.

The Cryptocurrency Wallet

A *cryptocurrency wallet* does not actually contain any cryptocurrency. Instead, it contains your private keys, which are the passwords needed to give you access to your cryptocurrencies. It is also used to send messages about transactions across the cryptocurrency network, either to transfer your cryptocurrency to another party or to create an address to be used by another party that wants to send cryptocurrency to you.

If you lose your private keys, then you no longer have access to your money. Instead, someone else who has gained access to these keys has control over the associated cryptocurrency. This means that access to the wallet must be tightly controlled through the use of two-factor authentication, encryption, strong passwords, and so forth.

Cryptocurrency Exchanges

A *cryptocurrency exchange* is an online web service that allows you to acquire cryptocurrencies, store them, and exchange them. When you set up a wallet on one of these exchanges and buy cryptocurrency through it, the result is that you own a small portion of that exchange's reserve of the applicable cryptocurrency, which the exchange tracks on your behalf. A variation on the concept is a *trading platform*, where the exchange connects buyers with sellers, and holds funds in escrow until the underlying transaction has been completed. A centralized cryptocurrency exchange tends to provide more liquidity for your funding than a trading platform, because fewer parties trade on a trading platform.

While some exchange users keep their digital assets within an exchange, this opens them up to hacking attacks. A safer approach is to move assets out of an exchange as quickly as possible, and retain them in a wallet.

Crypto Credit Cards

A few credit cards allow their cardholders to earn rewards in a cryptocurrency, rather than in the more traditional points, miles, or cash back. There are many variations on the concept, but the basic approach is to redeem rewards in crypto at the end of each month. Some of these cards charge a transaction fee in order to convert rewards to cryptocurrency. In some cases, the awarded cryptocurrency is held within a custodial account; it cannot be shifted into your own wallet. If a custodial account is used, then you can eventually choose to sell them in order to redeem a statement credit. A transaction fee is generally charged when you sell the cryptocurrency from the custodial account.

Crypto Wages

Some employees insist on being paid their wages in a cryptocurrency. The payment made is for the net wages of the person (after all payroll taxes and other withholdings), which is then converted into the cryptocurrency that the two parties have agreed to use. These payments are typically made through a payroll service that specializes in cryptocurrency payroll payments, where the employer pays this outside service. There is a monthly fee for the service, as well as a percentage charge (usually 2%) for the payments made with a cryptocurrency.

> **Note:** The Fair Labor Standards Act mandates that wages be paid in cash or a negotiable instrument that is payable at par – and cryptocurrency is neither one. So... crypto wages may not be legal.

Initial Coin Offerings

An *initial coin offering* (ICO) is an event where a business sells a new cryptocurrency to raise money. Investors receive cryptocurrency in exchange for their financial contributions. In most ICOs, investors are required to pay using another cryptocurrency, such as Ethereum or Bitcoin, though cash may also be accepted. The investment process involves sending money to a designated crypto wallet; investors provide their own recipient address to receive the crypto they have purchased. This approach is similar to what a business uses in an initial public offering, but it is quite unregulated, and so is more likely to result in losses.

What is Cryptocurrency Mining?

Not all cryptocurrencies require mining. But for those that do, cryptocurrency miners (computer system operators) download the applicable mining software for a cryptocurrency and run complex calculations that create new cryptocurrency, which are then added to the blockchain ledger. If they choose to do so, miners then sell their earnings[2]

---

[2] We are oversimplifying the situation. When new cryptocurrency is created, a *block subsidy* is paid to the miner for each block successfully added to the blockchain ledger. In addition, a

in order to pay for their operating costs and earn a profit. In essence, cryptocurrency miners are increasing the money supply for the market.

There are two methods that can be used to create cryptocurrency, which are as follows:

- *Proof of work method.* Under this approach, a miner is required to complete a computational task (such as completing a mathematical puzzle), with the first miner doing so being allowed to add a block to the blockchain and earn the associated fees. The odds of successfully completing the computational task increase when a miner has assembled a substantial amount of computing power – which increases the fixed asset base of the business. The main downside of this approach is the vast amount of electricity needed to complete the required computational tasks. It also tends to result in a relatively small number of transactions being processed per minute.

- *Proof of stake method.* Under this approach, the underlying cryptocurrency software chooses which cryptocurrency node will add the next block. In order to be in this group of nodes from which the selection will be made, the node operator must own a certain amount of the cryptocurrency throughout the mining process. The selection method used is based on the amount of the holder's stake and a random selection. In other words, the more cryptocurrency you own, the better the chance that you will be selected.[3] This approach makes it quite unlikely that anyone would want to submit improper transactions to the system, since doing so would result in the loss of the miner's stake. Also, given the greatly reduced cost of required mining rigs, transaction fees are much lower. This approach requires much less computing power than the proof of work method, and so requires less electricity.

The basic process for a miner is to generate new currency, validate it, collect these transactions into a new block, add the block to the ledger, and broadcast the new block to the cryptocurrency node network.

For some cryptocurrency, there is no mining, since the currency was pre-mined before it was launched. Instead, miners validate transactions and add them to blocks, which are then added to the blockchain – in exchange for a transaction fee.

> **Note:** The proof of work concept is a good way to keep malicious transactions from being submitted to a cryptocurrency network, which would slow it down to a crawl. If the amount of work required to submit a transaction is high, it becomes inordinately cost-*in*effective for someone to submit such a transaction.

---

fee is paid by each party spending the currency to have it added to the blockchain, which is paid to the miner.

[3] An alternative proof of stake method is for the selection to be from a queue of preselected miners.

Transaction Fees

You will incur a network fee when you send a cryptocurrency payment to another party – though this arrangement varies, depending on the type of cryptocurrency used. The fee charged will depend on the size of the transaction message and the extent to which the network is congested with transactions. The amount of the fee goes to the miner that adds the transaction to the applicable blockchain. The amount of this fee may be suggested by the wallet (again, depending on the type of cryptocurrency). If you want a lower fee, it may take a long time for the transaction to be completed; paying a higher fee accelerates the process. A miner that accepts this transaction will forward the requested amount to a third party and keep the pre-determined transaction fee.

Cryptocurrencies are frequently acquired and sold through a cryptocurrency exchange. The fees charged will vary by exchange, but a reasonable amount to expect is a 1% fee to convert cryptocurrency to cash, as well as standard network[4] fees. Or, if the exchange operates as a trading platform, then it earns money by charging a percentage of the total transaction.

> **Note:** Depending on the cryptocurrency exchange used, a transaction within the exchange involving someone else with an exchange account is typically free.

As an alternative, cryptocurrency can be purchased from an ATM. When you purchase from an ATM, it will accept cash or a debit from your bank account, and issue a receipt in exchange that contains a voucher number that is used to redeem the selected cryptocurrency. The purchasing fee ranges from 7% to 20%, with the fee comprised of a transaction fee and a blockchain (miner) fee. The exchange rate offered on these transactions tends to be poor, resulting in less cryptocurrency being purchased than would be the case with other methods.

Cryptocurrency Miner Revenues and Costs

Cryptocurrency miners incur a specific set of costs that are unique to this industry. They have to pay for computer hardware, which is typically loaded with expensive high-speed processing chips (known as Application-Specific Integrated Circuits, or ASICs). They also need extensive cooling systems to keep their hardware from overheating, which in turn requires significant ongoing electricity costs. They also need to maintain fast and highly reliable Internet connections with low latency and high bandwidth, in order to communicate with the cryptocurrency network. We delve into these and other aspects of miner costs in the following sub-sections.

---

[4] A variation on the network fee is the *gas fee*, which is charged by the Ethereum network. A transaction initiator pays this fee so that miners will have an incentive to process their transactions. A transaction with a high maximum gas price is more likely to attract a miner, who then selects it to include in the Ethereum blockchain.

Pool Mining

A significant investment in mining equipment is needed under the proof of work concept, to the extent that many smaller miners prefer to pool their resources and split the rewards of their combined efforts, based on their contributions to the pool. For example, a miner that contributes eight percent of the resources to a pool mining operation would be allocated eight percent of any resulting revenues. The accounting for resources contributed and payouts is based on the period of time during which a block is being mined by the pool; this period can range from just a few minutes to many hours. Payouts are made in the form of a cryptocurrency transfer to your wallet.

In this arrangement, a single pool operator manages the network node, while the pool members merely provide the processing power of their computer systems to the operation – which makes this a much easier option for a miner who would otherwise work alone.

The cost of pool mining is the depreciation on a miner's computer equipment, other costs of operations, and the fee charged by the pool operator in order to support its operations. This fee is likely to be in the form of a bigger cut of revenues generated, rather than a fee charged to the pool members. Alternatively, a pool operator might only allow you to share in the block subsidy, but not any transaction fees.

Cloud Mining

Under a *cloud mining* arrangement, a miner leases data center space from a mining farm, rather than owning the assets directly. Depending on how the arrangement is structured, a miner might be more accurately described as an investor, who is paid a portion of the proceeds.

Electricity Cost

One of the most significant expenses associated with proof-of-work cryptocurrency mining is electricity. Since mining is a competitive business, those miners that find the cheapest sources of electricity are more likely to prosper. These sources include underutilized hydroelectric dams, methane being flared from oil wells, and excess power generated by solar farms during periods of the day when consumption levels would otherwise be low. Some miners install solar panels on the premises to reduce the cost of electricity coming from outside providers; if so, this is a capitalized expense that is depreciated over the useful life of the panels.

Hardware Costs

The main hardware cost for a miner is the ASIC units. These are typically configured to be rack mountable, which means that a set of racks must also be purchased. Racks are not expensive, but a number of them may be required.

One of the problems with cryptocurrency mining is that the latest ASICs are needed in order to conduct calculations at a sufficiently rapid clip to generate a reasonable return on investment. In addition, the most recent ASICs can operate with less electricity, making older models less efficient to operate. This means that the useful life of an ASIC mining rig is likely to be only a few years (typically no more than four), after which it must be replaced.

A mining rig also needs power delivery units (PDUs) to route power from electrical outlets to power supply units. A PDU also protects against circuit overload. A power supply unit converts AC electricity to DC electricity, and then distributes it to the ASIC mining rig. The services of an electrician may need to be included in these costs, as well as an upgrade to your breaker panel, to ensure that it can handle the increased load from the mining gear.

Software Costs

The cost of software is generally not a concern for the miner, since mining software is usually downloadable for free. Also, ASIC hardware may already have mining software installed on it. However, some of this software is open source, in which case a donation can be made to support the continuing development of the software. Other software is free for small installations, but mandates a monthly fee for larger rigs.

Data Center Costs

At a more expanded level, a cryptocurrency mining operation might be contained within a data center, which may range in size from a shipping container to a warehouse. A variation on the concept is to set up a mining operation within a colocation center, which is already configured with sufficient power, Internet connections, and air conditioning. Using a colocation center is more common, since the infrastructure costs can be split among several clients.

Maintenance Costs

A key element of any mining operation will be fan replacement. Fans must operate 24/7 at high speed in order to pull heat away from mining equipment, and so are likely to fail at intervals. There is a lesser risk that ASIC boards will fail and require replacement.

Investing in Cryptocurrencies

Many people invest in cryptocurrencies – indeed, a central use case of cryptocurrencies is to speculate in changes in their value. Historically, cryptocurrencies have proven to have highly volatile valuations (partially due to the hype associated with them), so there will likely be substantial capital gains or losses on any investments made. A further concern is that some cryptocurrencies vanish entirely – along with your investment. In addition, some cryptocurrencies issue dividends, which generate dividend income.

The Internal Revenue Service views cryptocurrencies as property, so any gains experienced from holding them are subject to the capital gains tax.

Accounting for Cryptocurrency

We will now address the accounting topics associated with cryptocurrency. The information presented in the following pages is based on Accounting Standards Update 2023-08, *Intangibles—Goodwill and Other— Crypto Assets*, as well as the *Accounting for and Auditing of Digital Assets* practice aid, as issued by the AICPA and CIMA.

Evolving Treatment of Crypto Assets

The initial accounting treatment of crypto assets revolved around whether crypto assets should be treated as a form of cash. The accounting standards mandate that a *cash equivalent* must be a short-term, highly liquid investment that is readily convertible into a known amount of cash, and which is subject to an insignificant risk of changes in value. In the *Accounting for an Auditing of Digital Assets* practice aid, the case was made that crypto assets did not meet these criteria (given their volatility), and instead should be classified as intangible assets under Generally Accepted Accounting Principles. If classified as an intangible asset, cryptocurrencies would be recorded at their acquisition cost, and written down if their market values subsequently declined. There would be no opportunity to increase the recorded value of crypto assets under this approach. There was a great deal of pushback to this accounting treatment, since increases in the value of crypto assets would not appear in the holder's financial statements until these assets were sold. Consequently, ASU 2023-08 altered the original accounting treatment, so that crypto assets can now be recorded at fair value.

The new treatment mandated within ASU 2023-08 applies for crypto assets that meet all of the following criteria:

- Meets the definition of an intangible asset[5];
- Does not provide the holder with rights to or claims on any goods or services;
- Are created or reside on a distributed ledger that is based on a blockchain;
- Are secured through cryptography;
- Are fungible; and
- Are not created by the reporting entity.

The holder must measure these assets at their fair values in each reporting period, with any changes in fair value being recognized in net income.

The accounting treatment of crypto assets under International Financial Reporting Standards (IFRS) is about the same, since it allows use of the revaluation model (which is covered later in this manual). Under the revaluation option, you can revalue an intangible asset to its fair value in other comprehensive income, and record losses directly in earnings. That approach allows you to record upward swings in value.

What about a cryptocurrency that has been issued by a legitimate government? At this point, very few such currencies have been issued, including the Bahamian

---

[5] An intangible asset is one that lacks physical substance

SandDollar, the Jamaican JAM-DEX, and the Nigerian e-Naira[6]. Those cryptocurrencies that are direct liabilities of a central bank, and which are backed by a country's foreign reserves will likely be classified as cash equivalents, rather than intangible assets. That being the case, the accounting would be the same as for any other currency transactions you might have.

EXAMPLE

An American company enters into a transaction to pay 50,000 of the (mythical) Canadian government-backed PUCK-DEX cryptocurrency to a Canadian manufacturer in exchange for 1,000 pints of Canadian syrup. At the point of sale, the exchange rate is five PUCK-DEXs for every one U.S. dollar, so the purchaser records the seller's invoice as $10,000. Payment is due in one month. But on the payment date, the exchange rate has changed, so the buyer has to pay $11,000 to the seller. In this case, the extra $1,000 paid is recorded as a foreign currency loss.

Acquisition of Cryptocurrency

When you acquire cryptocurrency (such as through an exchange), record it at its cost. This cost includes all transaction costs or fees associated with the acquisition. Conversely, when you receive cryptocurrency from a customer as payment for a good or service, then the value of the asset received is initially measured at its fair value on the contract inception date. Any subsequent changes in the fair value of the cryptocurrency do not impact the amount of revenue recognized from the sale transaction.

If you acquire cryptocurrency via a business combination, then recognize it at its fair value as of the acquisition date.

Sales of Cryptocurrency

When you sell cryptocurrency to a customer (i.e., when the sale of cryptocurrency is part of your ordinary activities), then the proceeds are presented as revenue in the income statement. Conversely, if the sale is not to a customer, then you instead recognize a gain or loss on the sale transaction (net of cost), rather than revenue. All gains and losses recognized from the sale of cryptocurrency should be presented within the operating income section of the income statement.

Tracking of Cost Basis

The owner of crypto assets should track the cost of the units held, if those units were acquired at different times and different prices. This cost per unit can then be used to determine the cost at which units are eventually sold. Since it may not be possible to identify exactly which units were sold in specific transactions, you should employ a reasonable methodology for tracking these costs, such as the first-in, first-out or last-in, first-out method.

---

[6] Source: https://www.atlanticcouncil.org/cbdctracker

EXAMPLE

Sarah purchases 100 units of AccountingCoin in April at $10 each, and another 100 units in May at $9 each. She then sells 120 units. She has chosen to track costs using the first-in, first-out method, so the cost of the units sold is $1,180 (calculated as 100 units × $10, plus 20 units × $9).

Recognition of Cryptocurrency When Using a Third Party Hosted Wallet Service

When you hold cryptocurrency in a third-party hosted wallet service, is it recognized on your financial statements or those of the custodian? The rule is that the entity having control over the asset gets to recognize it. The concept of control can be difficult to pin down, can depend on a number of factors, and may require an attorney's analysis of the custodial agreement. The following are some of the factors outlined by FASB that may need to be reviewed when coming to a conclusion:

- Do any pertinent laws or regulations specify who is the owner?
- Does the underlying agreement specify whether title or legal ownership passes to the custodian?
- Does the custodian have the right to sell, transfer, loan, or pledge the cryptocurrency without your consent or notice?
- In the event of the custodian's bankruptcy, would the cryptocurrency be isolated from its creditors?
- Can you withdraw the cryptocurrency at any time and for any reason?
- Is the cryptocurrency held in a multi-signature wallet, and if so, which signatures are required to complete a transaction? Who controls the private keys to this wallet?
- Does the custodian commingle the cryptocurrencies of its depositors?

If an analysis of these factors (and others) concludes that the custodian should recognize the cryptocurrency in its financial statements, then the custodian should recognize the cryptocurrency as its assets in its financial statements, as well as an offsetting liability to return the cryptocurrency to you.

Accounting for Cryptocurrency Mining

There are two general accounting areas associated with cryptocurrency mining. The first is how to account for ongoing operations, for which the accounting is noted in the following bullet points:

- *Equipment.* Any ASICs, racks, power delivery units, breaker panels, cooling units, and the labor associated with assembling them can be capitalized. This can be a substantial sum when a miner wants to run the entire operation in-house, or through a pooling arrangement. As noted earlier, ASICs tend to become less cost-effective over time, so they should probably be depreciated over a period of about four years.

- *Equipment replacements.* The costs of equipment replacements can be capitalized, depending on whether they exceed the corporate capitalization limit. If not, these expenditures are charged to expense in the period incurred. Also, if an equipment replacement *is* capitalized, this implies that the remaining carrying amount of any equipment being replaced should now be written off.
- *Electricity.* The monthly electricity bill will be substantial, and should certainly be charged to expense in the period incurred; there is no reasonable justification for capitalizing this cost, since the cost incurred does not benefit future periods.
- *Pooling arrangement.* There are many variations on how the accounting can be conducted for a pooling arrangement, but the most likely approach is when the pool operator is conducting operations on behalf of the pool participants, who can recognize revenue (a credit) and an offsetting intangible asset (a debit) when they are apportioned transaction fees and block subsidies by the pool operator.
- *Cloud mining.* A cloud mining business will charge a standard rate, which should be charged to expense as incurred. In this case, the mining rigs of the cloud mining operation are being used, so there is no asset investment to be capitalized.
- *Colocation center.* A colocation center will charge a monthly fixed rate to use a portion of its facilities, as well as a variable rate that is based on electricity and Internet usage. In both cases, these amounts are charged to expense as incurred.

EXAMPLE

Luca Corporation contributes the services of its mining rig to a pool operator for the month of June. During this month, the pool participants cumulatively garner the group 1,500 PacioliCoin (named after the inventor of double entry accounting) from block subsidies and network fees. An examination of the situation reveals that the pool participants were generating this revenue from the provision of services to the pool operator's customers. Based on its proportion of the total processing power contributed to the pool, Luca Corporation is allocated 600 of the PacioliCoin. The fair value of this allocation is $28,000, based on the PacioliCoin-to-U.S. dollar exchange rate on the allocation date.

EXAMPLE

Anthony pays $5,000 per month to a prominent cloud mining operation for 125 MH/s[7]. He records this as an operating expense in the month paid, while the cloud mining operation records it at the end of that month as revenue on services rendered. The cloud mining operation then tallies the block subsidies and network fees generated during the month and sends a portion of it to Anthony in the applicable cryptocurrency, based on his proportion of the total

---

[7] MegaHashes per second, which is the rate at which a computer can produce a new hash, which will be used to create and secure the next block on a blockchain

MH/s paid during that period. Anthony records the received currency as revenue (a credit) at the exchange rate on the date received, as well as an intangible asset (a debit). Meanwhile, the cloud mining operation records this distribution as a reduction of its revenue (a debit) and a reduction of its cryptocurrency intangible asset (a credit).

The second general accounting area for cryptocurrency miners is how to account for the resulting network fees and block subsidies, which are paid in cryptocurrency. Transaction fees should be recognized as revenue from customers as soon as they have been earned, using the cryptocurrency-to-dollars exchange rate on the date earned. Transaction fees are stated in each transaction request and paid by the requesting party to the miner in exchange for the miner's processing of the transaction. Since the requester has contracted with the miner to obtain a service that is provided by the miner as part of its ordinary activities, this can be considered a sale of services to a customer. The timing of revenue recognition should be when the miner has successfully validated the customer's transaction in the blockchain. The fee paid is in cryptocurrency, which is considered a form of non-cash consideration. It is measured at its estimated fair value as of the contract inception date.

Any block rewards earned are usually recognized as revenue, as long as the related mining activities represent a contract with a customer to provide services (which is nearly always the case).

All of the preceding accounting issues for a cryptocurrency miner can be handled by employing the chart of accounts that appears in the following exhibit. We have not included in the chart any of the more generic accounts, such as cash, accounts payable, accrued liabilities, equity, and so forth.

Cryptocurrency Miner Chart of Accounts

Account Name	Account Inclusions
Fixed assets – mining hardware	Includes ASICs, racks, power delivery units, breaker panels, cooling units, and the labor associated with assembling them
Intangible assets – cryptocurrency holdings	Includes all cryptocurrency currently held by the business
Revenue – network fees and block subsidies	Includes all recognized revenue from network fees and block subsidies, including allocations from cloud mining and pool mining operators
Cloud mining expense	Includes the periodic fee charged by a cloud mining operator
Colocation expense	Includes the fixed and variable fees charged by a colocation operator
Depreciation – mining hardware	Includes the monthly depreciation charge on all capitalized mining hardware
Electricity expense	Includes the electricity expense incurred by the operation
Gain or loss on change in fair value of cryptocurrency asset	Includes the gain or loss recognized when the fair value of a crypto asset changes

The Revaluation Model

If it is possible to measure the fair value of a cryptocurrency asset reliably on an active market, there is an option under International Financial Reporting Standards to carry the asset at its revalued amount. Subsequent to revaluation, the amount carried on the books is the fair value, less subsequent impairment losses. Under this approach, continue to revalue the cryptocurrency asset at sufficiently regular intervals to ensure that the carrying amount does not differ materially from the fair value in any period.

If the revaluation model is initially used and it is later found that there is no longer an active market from which to derive a revaluation (such as when the cryptocurrency is no longer sold through a cryptocurrency exchange), subsequently use the last revalued amount as the carrying amount, less any accumulated impairment losses for the periods since the last revaluation. It is possible that the termination of an active market indicates that the value of the asset has been impaired, which may call for impairment testing.

If the election is made to use the revaluation model and a revaluation results in an increase in the carrying amount of a crypto asset, recognize the increase in other comprehensive income, as well as accumulate it in equity in an account entitled "revaluation surplus." However, if the increase reverses a revaluation decrease for the same asset that had been previously recognized in profit or loss, recognize the revaluation gain in profit or loss to the extent of the previous loss (thereby erasing the loss). If a revaluation results in a decrease in the carrying amount of an intangible asset, recognize the decrease in profit or loss. However, if there is a credit balance in the revaluation surplus for that asset, recognize the decrease in other comprehensive income to offset the credit balance. The decrease recognized in other comprehensive income decreases the amount of any revaluation surplus already recorded in equity. The following table summarizes the proper recognition of revaluation changes just described.

Revaluation Change Recognition

Asset Revaluation Change	Recognition
Value increases	Recognize in other comprehensive income and in the "revaluation surplus" equity account
Value increases, and reverses a prior revaluation decrease	Recognize gain in profit or loss to the extent of the previous loss, with the remainder in other comprehensive income
Value decreases	Recognize in profit or loss
Value decreases, but there is a credit in the revaluation surplus	Recognize in other comprehensive income to the extent of the credit, with the remainder in profit or loss

In essence, the international standards require the prominent display of any revaluation losses, and gives less reporting stature to revaluation gains. When the revaluation model is selected, it should be applied to an entire class of crypto assets; do not shift between the revaluation and cost models (where no revaluation is used) for individual cryptocurrencies within a class of assets. This rule does not apply when there is no active market for the assets, since it is then impossible to use the revaluation method.

Crypto Asset Disclosures

In addition to the accounting requirements noted earlier, the holder of crypto assets is also required to disclose the following information in the footnotes that accompany its financial statements:

<u>For Annual and Interim Reporting</u>

- The name, cost basis, fair value, and number of units for each significant crypto asset held. Also disclose the aggregate fair values and cost bases of all other crypto asset holdings that are not individually significant.
- If any crypto assets are subject to restrictions on their sale, disclose their fair value, the nature and remaining duration of the restriction, and triggering events that would cause the restriction to lapse.

<u>For Annual Reporting</u>

- An aggregated rollforward of all crypto asset holdings in the reporting period, including additions, sales, gains and losses. Gains and losses may come from periodic remeasurements of crypto assets, and should be reported on separate lines of the rollforward.
- For any crypto asset sales, disclose the difference between the cost basis and sale price, and describe the activities that resulted in these sales. For example, the description might state that assets were acquired from mining activities or purchases, while they may have been disposed of from sale transactions or by using them as payment for services.
- If you do not present gains and losses separately, then disclose the income statement line item in which they are recognized.
- The method used to determine the cost basis of the crypto assets[8].

> **Note:** An organization that receives crypto assets as noncash consideration or as a contribution, and then nearly immediately[9] converts them into cash does not have to include this activity in its crypto asset disclosures.

Crypto Asset Presentation

A holder of crypto assets must present them separately from other intangible assets in its balance sheet. Further, the holder must present any changes from fair value remeasurements separately from changes in the carrying amounts of other intangible assets in its income statement.

If an organization receives a donation of crypto assets and then converts them nearly immediately into cash, this should be classified as an operating cash flow on the entity's statement of cash flows. However, if the donation restricts the use of the

---

[8] Such as the first-in first-out method, the specific identification method, or the average cost method.

[9] Nearly immediately is defined as a within hours or a few days, rather than weeks.

donated assets for a long-term purpose, then the donation is instead classified as a financing activity.

Summary

There are several issues associated with the accounting for cryptocurrency. The first is that you must continually adjust the recorded amount of this asset to its fair value in each reporting period, and recognize a gain or loss on any changes. Second, it must be valued at the exchange rate at the point when the cryptocurrency is recognized, which requires that you identify the principal market for the cryptocurrency (where the exchange rate can be obtained). And finally, a crypto miner can recognize network fees and block subsidies as revenue (in most cases), while someone merely holding cryptocurrency must recognize a gain or loss (not revenue) when it is eventually sold.

Glossary

B

Bandwidth. The amount of data throughput through a medium of communication.

Block subsidy. An amount paid to a miner for each block successfully added to a blockchain ledger.

Blockchain. A distributed database that is shared among the nodes of a computer network.

C

Cash equivalent. A short-term, highly liquid investment that is readily convertible into a known amount of cash, and which is subject to an insignificant risk of changes in value.

Cloud mining. When a miner leases data center space from a mining farm, rather than owning the assets directly, and is then paid a portion of the proceeds.

Cryptocurrency. Any form of currency that exists digitally and uses cryptography to secure transactions.

Cryptocurrency exchange. An online web service that allows you to acquire cryptocurrencies, store them, and exchange them.

Cryptography. A method of protecting information and communications through the use of codes, so that only those for whom the information is intended can read and process it.

G

Gas fee. A fee paid by transaction initiators on the Ethereum network, so that miners will have an incentive to process their transactions.

I

Initial coin offering. An event where a business sells a new cryptocurrency to raise money.

L

Latency. The amount of time required for data to move from one point to another.

M

MegaHashes per second. The rate at which a computer can produce a new hash, which will be used to create and secure the next block on a blockchain.

Most advantageous market. The market that maximizes the amount that can be received from the sale of cryptocurrency, after deducting transaction costs.

N

Node. A computer that receives and validates transactions and blocks.

P

Pool mining. When miners pool their resources and split the rewards of their combined efforts, based on their contributions to the pool.

Principal market. The market with the greatest volume and level of activity for a cryptocurrency.

Proof of stake method. When the underlying cryptocurrency software chooses which cryptocurrency node will add the next block to a blockchain.

Proof of work method. When a miner is required to complete a computational task, with the first miner doing so being allowed to add a block to a blockchain and earn the fees associated with doing so.

T

Trading platform. A cryptocurrency exchange that connects buyers with sellers, and holds funds in escrow until the underlying transaction has been completed.

W

Wallet. A software program that allows you to store your cryptocurrency and allow for the sending and receiving of crypto transactions.

Index